Make the Most of the
New Year

Achievable Goals for
Health, Relationships, and *Faith*

MariLee Parrish

BARBOUR
PUBLISHING

© 2010 by Barbour Publishing, Inc.

Compiled by MariLee Parrish.

ISBN 978-1-60260-832-0

Published by Barbour Publishing, Inc., P.O. Box 719, Uhrichsville, Ohio 44683, www.barbourbooks.com

Our mission is to publish and distribute inspirational products offering exceptional value and biblical encouragement to the masses.

 Member of the
Evangelical Christian
Publishers Association

Printed in the United States of America.

Contents

INTRODUCTION

Happy New Year!

Most of us come up with at least one New Year's resolution every January. Some of us have lists! But few of us make it to February still plugging away at our goals. *Make the Most of the New Year* offers ideas and reminders to help you stay on track throughout the year. From eating right to making a difference in your community, you can do "all things through Christ who gives you strength!"

Many blessings for a wonderful year ahead,
MariLee Parrish

Make the Most of . . .*You*

I will make wise choices concerning my health.

Dear friend, I pray that you may enjoy good health and that all may go well with you, even as your soul is getting along well.

3 JOHN 2 NIV

I will practice self-control.

Therefore, prepare your minds for action;
be self-controlled; set your hope fully on the grace
to be given you when Jesus Christ is revealed.

1 PETER 1:13 NIV

I will be bold and
stand up for my faith.

*"Have I not commanded you? Be strong and courageous.
Do not be terrified; do not be discouraged, for the LORD
your God will be with you wherever you go."*

JOSHUA 1:9 NIV

Start the New Year right by committing all of your goals and plans to the Lord. Ask for His direction and guidance as you make plans for the coming year.

I will accept constructive criticism
and learn from it.

If you listen to constructive criticism,
you will be at home among the wise.
If you reject discipline, you only harm yourself; but if
you listen to correction, you grow in understanding.
PROVERBS 15:31–32 NLT

I will not spread gossip
or listen to rumors.

The gossip of bad people gets them in trouble;
the conversation of good people keeps them out of it.

PROVERBS 12:13 MSG

I will choose my words wisely.

The lips of the godly speak helpful words,
but the mouth of the wicked speaks perverse words.

PROVERBS 10:32 NLT

When we take our eyes off Christ for even a moment, it's easy to seek the applause of men rather than to live for God. Strive to keep your eyes on Christ in every moment.

I will work on having
a positive attitude.

*A cheerful look brings joy to the heart;
good news makes for good health.*

PROVERBS 15:30 NLT

I will surround myself with positive influences.

*Don't befriend angry people or associate with
hot-tempered people, or you will learn to
be like them and endanger your soul.*

PROVERBS 22:24–25 NLT

I will work on being humble
instead of vying for attention.

*"For everyone who exalts himself shall be humbled,
and he who humbles himself shall be exalted."*

LUKE 14:11 NASB

Dwelling constantly on past regrets will get you nowhere. Take some time and write down your list of regrets. Is there anything that you can make right? Offer your list to the Lord, make right what you can, and let the rest go.

I will be known as a
person of integrity.

*People with integrity walk safely, but those
who follow crooked paths will slip and fall.*

I will live each day to the fullest.

The thief comes only to steal and kill and destroy;
I have come that they may have life,
and have it to the full.

John 10:10 NIV

I will not dwell on the past,
but look forward to all that
God wants to do in my life.

*Jesus replied, "No one who puts his hand to the plow
and looks back is fit for service in the kingdom of God."*

LUKE 9:62 NIV

*G*et comfortable with sharing your faith. Write down several scriptures that mean the most to you and memorize them. Share your testimony by telling your story to those around you and by living out your faith each day.

I will go outside my comfort
zone to share my faith.

*When they finally found him, they begged him not to
leave them. But he replied, "I must preach the Good
News of the Kingdom of God in other towns, too,
because that is why I was sent."*

Luke 4:42–43 nlt

I will boast about the grace of God,
not about myself.

For it is by grace you have been saved, through faith—
and this not from yourselves, it is the gift of God—
not by works, so that no one can boast.

EPHESIANS 2:8–9 NIV

I will stop watching and listening to programs that are not edifying.

The good man brings good things out of the good stored up in his heart, and the evil man brings evil things out of the evil stored up in his heart. For out of the overflow of his heart his mouth speaks.

LUKE 6:45 NIV

*M*ake a commitment to severely limit your television intake. *If* something is off-limits to children, it's usually not a good idea for adults, either. *What goes* in always comes out.

I will honor God with my body.

Do you not know that your body is a temple of the Holy Spirit, who is in you, whom you have received from God? You are not your own; you were bought at a price. Therefore honor God with your body.

1 CORINTHIANS 6:19–20 NIV

I will no longer conform
to this world.

Do not conform any longer to the pattern of this world,
but be transformed by the renewing of your mind.
Then you will be able to test and approve what God's
will is—his good, pleasing and perfect will.

ROMANS 12:2 NIV

I will concentrate on what God
knows about me rather than what
other people think of me.

*Do not look on his appearance or on the height
of his stature.... For the LORD sees not as man
sees: man looks on the outward appearance,
but the LORD looks on the heart.*

1 SAMUEL 16:7 ESV

Choose to take better care of your health. Make wise choices when eating and planning the menu for the week. Get regular medical check-ups and exercise at least three times a week.

I will be content with the
possessions that I have.

*Keep your lives free from the love of money and be
content with what you have, because God has said,
"Never will I leave you; never will I forsake you."*

HEBREWS 13:5 NIV

I will learn how to be content
in every circumstance.

*I know what it is to be in need, and I know
what it is to have plenty. I have learned the secret
of being content in any and every situation.*

PHILIPPIANS 4:12 NIV

I will be thankful.

And let the peace of Christ rule in your hearts, to which indeed you were called in one body. And be thankful.

COLOSSIANS 3:15 ESV

Count your blessings. Make a list of all the things you are thankful for and post them in a prominent location as a reminder of how much you've been blessed.

I will admit when I am wrong.

He who conceals his transgressions
will not prosper, but he who confesses
and forsakes them will find compassion.

PROVERBS 28:13 NASB

I will give up bad habits and
ask for accountability.

*Jesus said to him, "If you can believe,
all things are possible to him who believes."*

MARK 9:23 NKJV

I will make the most of every opportunity.

Be very careful, then, how you live—not as unwise but as wise, making the most of every opportunity, because the days are evil. Therefore do not be foolish, but understand what the Lord's will is.

EPHESIANS 5:15–17 NIV

*Commit to better organization
in your home. Purchase a family
calendar and write down everything
that is scheduled. Update this
schedule on a weekly basis.*

I will not be a workaholic.

It's useless to rise early and go to bed late,
and work your worried fingers to the bone.
Don't you know he enjoys giving rest to those he loves?

Psalm 127:2 MSG

I will take my
responsibilities seriously.

Great gifts mean great responsibilities;
greater gifts, greater responsibilities!

LUKE 12:48 MSG

I will rely on God's power rather
than my own strength.

Be strong in the Lord and in his mighty power.
Put on all of God's armor so that you will be able
to stand firm against all strategies of the devil.

EPHESIANS 6:10–11 NLT

If you have a bad habit you need to overcome, talk to your accountability partner or pastor. With power from God and the support of friends and family, you can break free!

Make the Most of. . .
Your Relationships

I will seek the approval of God
rather than my peers.

*Your approval means nothing to me, because
I know you don't have God's love within you.*

JOHN 5:41–42 NLT

I will work more on listening rather than adding my "two cents."

Even a fool is thought wise if he keeps silent,
and discerning if he holds his tongue.

PROVERBS 17:28 NIV

I will respond gently
when I am angry.

*A gentle answer turns away wrath,
but a harsh word stirs up anger.*

PROVERBS 15:1 NIV

The Bible has a lot to say about our words. Be a bearer of good news to your family and friends instead of one who likes to share the latest bit of gossip or complain about your life.

I will be there for my friends
when they are in need.

A friend loves at all times,
and a brother is born for adversity.

PROVERBS 17:17 NASB

I will be a better friend.

*Be alert. If you see your friend going wrong,
correct him. If he responds, forgive him.*

LUKE 17:3 MSG

I will choose my friends wisely.

Do not be deceived:
"Evil company corrupts good habits."

1 CORINTHIANS 15:33 NKJV

True friendship is a gift from the Lord. It's important to "speak the truth in love" at all times with your friends. That's how authentic friendships are made.

I will pray for those who have
had a negative impact on me
and look for ways to bless them.

But to you who are willing to listen, I say,
love your enemies! Do good to those who hate you.

LUKE 6:27 NLT

I will forgive others and
never hold a grudge.

*Forgive us our sins, for we also forgive
everyone who sins against us.*

LUKE 11:4 NIV

I will love others and put their
needs above my own.

My command is this: Love each other as I have
loved you. Greater love has no one than this,
that he lay down his life for his friends.

*P*ray for godly friends. Your
"inner circle" of friends should
be positive, uplifting people.
Make sure those who are closest
to you have a positive influence
on your life and your family.

I will not be judgmental.

Do not judge, and you will not be judged.
Do not condemn, and you will not be condemned.
Forgive, and you will be forgiven.

LUKE 6:37 NIV

I will accept God's grace
and be gracious to others.

*But sin didn't, and doesn't, have a chance in competition
with the aggressive forgiveness we call grace. When it's
sin versus grace, grace wins hands down.*

ROMANS 5:20 MSG

I will respect and pray for
my boss and local authorities.

Everyone must submit to governing authorities. For all authority comes from God, and those in positions of authority have been placed there by God.

Romans 13:1 nlt

Learn to be more gracious to those around you. God extends His grace and mercy to us even though we don't deserve it. The next time you are tempted to judge someone else, stop and remember how much you have been forgiven.

I will pray for my spouse each day.

*And it is my prayer that your love may abound
more and more, with knowledge and all discernment,
so that you may approve what is excellent, and so
be pure and blameless for the day of Christ.*

PHILIPPIANS 1:9–10 ESV

I will pray for my
children each day.

These commandments that I give you today are to be
upon your hearts. Impress them on your children. Talk
about them when you sit at home and when you walk
along the road, when you lie down and when you get up.

DEUTERONOMY 6:6–7 NIV

I will pray for my unsaved friends
and family members each day.

*Confess your sins to each other and pray for each
other so that you may be healed. The earnest prayer
of a righteous person has great power and
produces wonderful results.*

JAMES 5:16 NLT

*P*lan a family council meeting. Make
your family's favorite dessert. Discuss
whatever needs to be addressed and
then talk about how you can spend
more time together as a family.

I will spend more time
with my family.

*For I have chosen him, so that he will direct his
children and his household after him to keep the way
of the Lord by doing what is right and just.*

I will ask for biblical and
professional advice when needed.

Fools are headstrong and do what they like;
wise people take advice.

PROVERBS 12:15 MSG

I will be a better parent.

Fathers, do not provoke your children to anger by the way you treat them. Rather, bring them up with the discipline and instruction that comes from the Lord.

EPHESIANS 6:4 NLT

Leave your work at work. When you are at home, be fully present with your family. If you work from home, set office hours and keep them.

I will treat others as
I want to be treated.

*So in everything, do to others what you would have them
do to you, for this sums up the Law and the Prophets.*

MATTHEW 7:12 NIV

I will promote love at all times.

He who covers over an offense promotes love, but
whoever repeats the matter separates close friends.

PROVERBS 17:9 NIV

I will ask the Lord to convict
me when I am being selfish.

If any of you wants to be my follower,
you must turn from your selfish ways,
take up your cross daily, and follow me.

LUKE 9:23 NLT

There are many wonderful resources available for parents to help raise godly children. Check with your church library or get a recommendation from Christian parents whom you respect.

I will invite Christ to be the center
of my life and my family.

*I pray that out of his glorious riches he may strengthen
you with power through his Spirit in your inner being,
so that Christ may dwell in your hearts through faith.*

EPHESIANS 3:16–17 NIV

I will plant the fruit of the Spirit in
the lives of those around me.

*But the Holy Spirit produces this kind of fruit in our
lives: love, joy, peace, patience, kindness, goodness,
faithfulness, gentleness, and self-control.*

GALATIANS 5:22–23 NLT

I will not be afraid to ask for help from God and others.

You do not have, because you do not ask God.

JAMES 4:2 NIV

*Start a new weekly tradition:
Discuss a favorite scripture with
your family or a trusted friend.*

I will keep my priorities straight.

*Many are the plans in a man's heart,
but it is the LORD's purpose that prevails.*

PROVERBS 19:21 NIV

I will not be anxious
about fitting in.

Do not be anxious about anything,
but in everything, by prayer and petition,
with thanksgiving, present your requests to God.

PHILIPPIANS 4:6 NIV

I will strive to be fair in my
judgment of others.

*"If any one of you is without sin,
let him be the first to throw a stone."*

John 8:7 niv

Make an effort to reconnect with old friends you've lost touch with. Life is busy and full of distractions, but it's important to set aside time to honor your friends and loved ones. Chances are, they miss talking to you, too!

Make the Most of. . .
Your Community

I will look for opportunities to give of myself without expecting anything in return.

Give to everyone who asks you, and if anyone takes what belongs to you, do not demand it back.

LUKE 6:30 NIV

I will acknowledge God in
everything I do.

Trust in the LORD *with all your heart and*
lean not on your own understanding;
in all your ways acknowledge him,
and he will make your paths straight.
PROVERBS 3:5–6 NIV

My mission will be to love
God and love others.

*" 'You must love the LORD your God with all your heart,
all your soul, all your strength, and all your mind.'
And, 'Love your neighbor as yourself.' "
"Right!" Jesus told him. "Do this and you will live!"*
LUKE 10:27–28 NLT

Jesus summed up the entire Bible by telling us to love God and love others. Look for ways to share God's love with those around you. Be intentional. Write down some ideas and go for it!

I will use my talent to serve God.

*To those who use well what they are given,
even more will be given, and they will have an
abundance. But from those who do nothing,
even what little they have will be taken away.*

MATTHEW 25:29 NLT

I will serve those in need
on a regular basis.

*But when you give a banquet, invite the poor,
the crippled, the lame, the blind, and you will be blessed.*

LUKE 14:13–14 NIV

I will give of my time and money to the less fortunate in my community.

He who gives to the poor will lack nothing,
but he who closes his eyes to them receives many curses.

PROVERBS 28:27 NIV

Worship isn't just about singing songs in church on Sunday. God wants us to live a life of everyday worship. You can start each day knowing that every task you undertake can be an offering of worship to God if you let it!

I will pray for more opportunities
to serve others.

He who oppresses the poor shows contempt for their
Maker, but whoever is kind to the needy honors God.

PROVERBS 14:31 NIV

I will share the message of the cross
with as many people as I can.

For God loved the world so much that he gave his
one and only Son, so that everyone who believes
in him will not perish but have eternal life.

JOHN 3:16 NLT

I will not be intimidated
when doing God's will.

*Because the Sovereign LORD helps me, I will
not be disgraced. Therefore, I have set my face
like a stone, determined to do his will. And I
know that I will not be put to shame.*

ISAIAH 50:7 NLT

We are each equipped with unique talents and abilities to serve the Lord. Having trouble figuring out yours? Meet with your pastor or spiritual mentor and have a heart-to-heart about your gifts and how you might use them to further God's kingdom.

I will not delay in doing what is right.

But encourage one another daily, as long as it is called Today, so that none of you may be hardened by sin's deceitfulness.

HEBREWS 3:13 NIV

I will not put off doing the things that need doing today.

How do you know what your life will be like tomorrow? Your life is like the morning fog—it's here a little while, then it's gone.

JAMES 4:14 NLT

I will stop procrastinating.

Farmers who wait for perfect weather never plant.
If they watch every cloud, they never harvest.

Ecclesiastes 11:4 nlt

*M*ake it a monthly habit to volunteer at your local soup kitchen or visit a nursing home. Do what you can to share the love of God with those in need. Contact your church to get involved with the needy in your area.

I will respect and pray for the leaders of my church.

Obey your leaders and submit to their authority. They keep watch over you as men who must give an account. Obey them so that their work will be a joy, not a burden, for that would be of no advantage to you.

HEBREWS 13:17 NIV

I will respect and pray
for my national leaders.

For the Lord's sake, respect all human authority—
whether the king as head of state, or the officials he has
appointed. For the king has sent them to punish those
who do wrong and to honor those who do right.

1 PETER 2:13–14 NLT

I will be a good example.

Don't let anyone look down on you because you are young, but set an example for the believers in speech, in life, in love, in faith and in purity.

1 TIMOTHY 4:12 NIV

*T*rials and problems are inevitable.
We can't choose our circumstances
but we can choose our attitude. Work
on staying positive in the midst
of trouble by reading God's Word
and applying it to your life. Seek
accountability in this area.

I will honor God with my time.

Teach us to number our days aright,
that we may gain a heart of wisdom.

PSALM 90:12 NIV

I will serve God with excellence.

Don't just do the minimum that will get you by.
Do your best. Work from the heart for your real Master,
for God. . . . Keep in mind always that the ultimate
Master you're serving is Christ.

COLOSSIANS 3:23–24 MSG

I will do the best I can with what I've been given.

By his divine power, God has given us everything we need for living a godly life. We have received all of this by coming to know him, the one who called us to himself by means of his marvelous glory and excellence.

2 PETER 1:3 NLT

Replace your self-confidence with "God-confidence" that comes only from knowing Christ more, renewing your mind through scripture, and allowing Him complete control over your life.

I will not be lazy.

Lazy hands make a man poor,
but diligent hands bring wealth.

PROVERBS 10:4 NIV

I will learn to be a better leader.

For the LORD gives wisdom, and from his mouth come knowledge and understanding.

PROVERBS 2:6 NIV

I will be a constant encouragement
to those around me.

*Don't use foul or abusive language. Let everything you
say be good and helpful, so that your words will be an
encouragement to those who hear them.*

EPHESIANS 4:29 NLT

*W*hile we don't have to
agree with government leaders
and those in authority over us,
we do have to treat them with respect
and love. Make a daily habit of
praying that they will turn to God
and make wise decisions.

I will not push my own agenda,
but will wait for the Lord.

Wait for the LORD; be strong and
take heart and wait for the LORD.

PSALM 27:14 NIV

I will pray for God's will and His
blessing in my mission work.

*Jabez cried out to the God of Israel, "Oh, that you
would bless me and enlarge my territory! Let your hand
be with me, and keep me from harm so that I will be
free from pain." And God granted his request.*

1 CHRONICLES 4:10 NIV

I will inspire others to live the Christian life and not give up.

Let us not become weary in doing good, for at the proper time we will reap a harvest if we do not give up.

GALATIANS 6:9 NIV

*S*ign up to serve at your church in whatever capacity is needed. You will develop deeper connections with people as you serve the Lord together.

I will accept God's
direction and guidance.

*Then Jesus went to work on his disciples.
"Anyone who intends to come with me has to let
me lead. You're not in the driver's seat; I am."*

MATTHEW 16:24 MSG

I will promote a life of worship.

But the time is coming—indeed it's here now—
when true worshipers will worship the Father in
spirit and in truth. The Father is looking for
those who will worship him that way.

JOHN 4:23 NLT

I will listen for and acknowledge
God's call on my life.

*But the one who hears my words and does not
put them into practice is like a man who built a
house on the ground without a foundation.*

LUKE 6:49 NIV

As Christians, we should strive to honor God with our time, talent, and treasure. Brainstorm ways to give more of yourself in these areas.

Make the Most of. . .
Your Faith

I will start each day with the Lord, committing all my plans to Him.

Commit to the LORD whatever you do,
and your plans will succeed.

PROVERBS 16:3 NIV

I will make more time
for focused prayer.

As often as possible Jesus withdrew to
out-of-the-way places for prayer.

LUKE 5:16 MSG

I will live my life for
God instead of myself.

*Whoever tries to keep his life will lose it,
and whoever loses his life will preserve it.*

LUKE 17:33 NIV

Set up a family budget that honors the Lord. Remember that it is God's money that He is allowing you to use. Use it for His glory.

I will listen for His still,
small voice in my life.

"I am the good shepherd; I know my sheep
and my sheep know me—just as the Father
knows me and I know the Father—and I
lay down my life for the sheep."

John 10:14–15 NIV

I will honor God with my finances.

Honor God with everything you own;
give him the first and the best. Your barns
will burst, your wine vats will brim over.

PROVERBS 3:9–10 MSG

I will run to the Lord first
when I have a problem,
before calling a friend.

The name of the LORD is a strong tower;
the righteous run to it and are safe.

<small>PROVERBS 18:10 NIV</small>

Many times when a problem
arises, our first thought is to call
up a friend and get advice. While
wise counsel is good, get in the habit
of taking your concerns to your
Heavenly Counselor first.

I will spend dedicated time
with the Lord each day.

*Remain in me, and I will remain in you. No branch
can bear fruit by itself; it must remain in the vine.
Neither can you bear fruit unless you remain in me.*

JOHN 15:4 NIV

I will follow after God faithfully.

Let love and faithfulness never leave you;
bind them around your neck, write them on
the tablet of your heart. Then you will win favor
and a good name in the sight of God and man.

PROVERBS 3:3–4 NIV

I will seek wisdom
from God's Word.

Wise choices will watch over you. Understanding will keep you safe. Wisdom will save you from evil people, from those whose words are twisted.

PROVERBS 2:11–12 NLT

*F*ind an accountability partner
whom you can meet with to discuss
your faith and grow in Christ together.
Make a list of areas that need
addressing in your life and ask each
other the tough questions every week.

I will worry less and
trust God more.

*Then Jesus said to his disciples: "Therefore I tell you,
do not worry about your life, what you will eat; or about
your body, what you will wear. Life is more than food,
and the body more than clothes."*

LUKE 12:22–23 NIV

When I start to worry, I will
confess this to the Lord and pray.

Can all your worries add a single moment to your life?
And if worry can't accomplish a little thing like that,
what's the use of worrying over bigger things?

LUKE 12:25–26 NLT

I will relax and let God have
control of all things.

The Master said, "Martha, dear Martha,
you're fussing far too much and getting yourself
worked up over nothing. One thing only is essential,
and Mary has chosen it—it's the main course,
and won't be taken from her."

LUKE 10:41–42 MSG

Jesus wants to be the very center of everything we do and everything we are. Instead of placing Him at the top of your to-do list to be checked off for the day, invite Him to be a part of every moment.

I will trust God to care for my needs.

*Seek the Kingdom of God above all else,
and he will give you everything you need.*

LUKE 12:31 NLT

I will pray continually
and never give up.

*Then Jesus told his disciples a parable to show them
that they should always pray and not give up.*

My faith will grow this year.

And the Lord said, "If you had faith like a mustard seed, you would say to this mulberry tree, 'Be uprooted and be planted in the sea'; and it would obey you."

LUKE 17:6 NASB

God says that His Word is "living and active." The Word of God has the power to change lives. Consider reading through the entire Bible this year.

I will go to church regularly.

*Let us not give up meeting together, as some are in the
habit of doing, but let us encourage one another—and
all the more as you see the Day approaching.*

HEBREWS 10:25 NIV

I will seek the presence of
God in the midst of trouble.

*"I have told you all this so that you may have peace in
me. Here on earth you will have many trials and sorrows.
But take heart, because I have overcome the world."*

John 16:33 nlt

I will be patient and faithful
as God works in my life.

And the seeds that fell on the good soil represent honest,
good-hearted people who hear God's word, cling to it,
and patiently produce a huge harvest.

LUKE 8:15 NLT

*Make a prayer list and keep
it in your car. As you run errands
or drive to work, you can pray
(with your eyes open, of course!)
for everyone on your list.*

I will read a proverb everyday.

*These are the proverbs of Solomon,
David's son, king of Israel. Their purpose is
to teach people wisdom and discipline, to help
them understand the insights of the wise.*

PROVERBS 1:1–2 NLT

I will seek the Lord
with all my heart.

*"God did this so that men would seek him and
perhaps reach out for him and find him, though he
is not far from each one of us. 'For in him we
live and move and have our being.'"*

ACTS 17:27–28 NIV

When I feel afraid, I will find
strength in God.

Indeed, the very hairs of your head are all numbered.
Don't be afraid; you are worth more
than many sparrows.

LUKE 12:7 NIV

One way to grow in faith is to start studying the Bible. Call your church and ask about Bible studies you can join. If there isn't one going on right now, pray about starting your own.

I will trust God's will for my life.

"I am the Lord's servant," Mary answered.
"May it be to me as you have said."
Then the angel left her.

LUKE 1:38 NIV

I will remember that
God is always with me.

*Teach these new disciples to obey all the commands
I have given you. And be sure of this: I am with you
always, even to the end of the age.*

MATTHEW 28:20 NLT

I will trust God with
my dreams and goals.

LORD, sustain me as you promised, that I may live!
Do not let my hope be crushed.

PSALM 119:116 NLT

Jesus tells us that if we want to bear fruit, we must "remain in Him." Spend some time reading and meditating on John chapter 15 to learn more about what this means.

I'll focus on God's truths when
I'm facing difficult times.

*For his anger lasts only a moment, but his favor
lasts a lifetime; weeping may remain for a night,
but rejoicing comes in the morning.*

PSALM 30:5 NIV

I will give my insecurities
to the Lord.

For God has not given us a spirit of fear and timidity,
but of power, love, and self-discipline.

2 TIMOTHY 1:7 NLT

I will begin with the end in mind.

*Forgetting the past and looking forward to what
lies ahead, I press on to reach the end of the race
and receive the heavenly prize for which God,
through Christ Jesus, is calling us.*

PHILIPPIANS 3:13–14 NLT

We only make things worse when we worry and try to control things that are out of our hands. Life gets simpler when we let God be God. Take a deep breath and choose to trust that God knows what He's doing.

Scripture Index